True You
A GENDER JOURNEY

Clarion Books
An *Imprint of HarperCollinsPublishers*

By Gwen Agna and Shelley Rotner   Photographs by Shelley Rotner

We are kids!

Girls, boys,
neither,
both,
or just not sure.

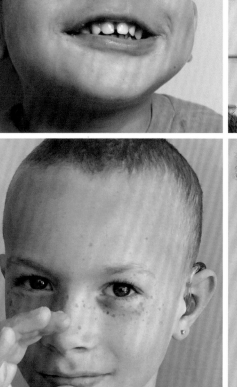

We are courageous,

curious, creative, and proud.

We are joyful,

strong,

loving and kind.

There are different ways
to show and be
who you are.

It's up to you—

how you feel,

how you dress,

how you act,

how you play,

learn, and love.

People might think your body is
a clue to who you are.

It is what *you* think that matters!

As you grow older, you might change
how you feel about who you are.

There's a whole wide world of kids
and different ways to be who you are—
your true you.

They thought I was a boy when I was born. But now, sometimes I feel like a girl.

Everyone can dress however they want.

Boys can wear dresses and girls don't have to.

When I was born,
people said I was a girl.
They were right!

**I'm a girl because
I feel like a girl!**

People should love everybody for who
they are. Anyone can play with dolls.
All the colors are for everyone.
Everybody can be strong.

Who decided there should be words like boy and girl anyway?

Sometimes in the morning I feel like a she, and later the same day I feel like a he even though they thought I was a girl when I was born.

But it's all right to change how you feel in the day.

Whether you go by he, she, they, or ze, everyone is in charge of their pronouns and what they like to be called. Everyone should be respected for who they are!

I'm not sure if I'm a boy or a girl.

Sometimes it's hard to know how I feel or what to wear.

It doesn't matter. I'm a kid.

I like my bunny and cars.

Even though they thought I was a boy when I was born, I'm not. I'm a girl. **I just know I am a girl because I feel like one inside.**

Everyone thought I was a girl when I was born. But I'm really a boy! People should NOT be treated differently because of their gender. **Everyone should feel safe to be who they are.**

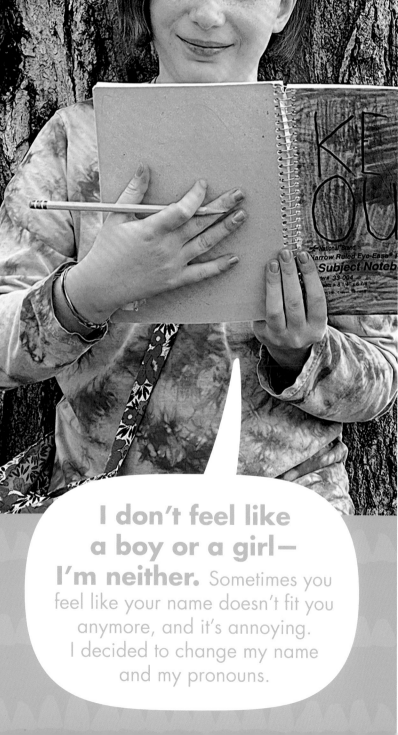

Sometimes it's hard when kids say you have to be a boy or a girl when you're not. **Everyone should feel safe to just be who they are.**

When I was born, they thought I was a boy. I am!

I have all kinds of friends.

What matters is if you're nice and kind to everyone.

I love my sibling. People should have the choice of what they want to be and shouldn't be judged for that. Nonbinary kids, like my sibling, should be treated the same way that other friends who are cisgender boys or girls are treated. **We're all people.**

Having a sibling that respects and supports me is awesome!

I can be myself with her.
She brings love into my life.

exploring different things!

We are all kinds of kids— siblings, sisters, and brothers.

We are sons, daughters, children, niblings, and grandchildren. And friends!

. . . whoever we want to be.

But How?
For Kids Finding Out Who They Are

In this book you read about other children, many of whom are like you. They look like you and have thoughts and ideas that you are having. Perhaps you feel that people think you are a boy or a girl when you are not. Sometimes you want to wear different clothes or act in a different way. That's okay! As we saw with the children on these pages, it's okay to be different than what others might think.

But how?

First, talk to an adult that you trust—your parents or others who take care of you. Tell them how you feel. Tell them if your feelings are making you sad or happy. Ask them to help you feel good about yourself by talking to others—your teacher or other parents. You may want to tell them about this book and about the children and their stories. You may want to ask your school librarian if there are books in the library about transgender children.

Always remember that just like the children in this book, you are a special child. Your thoughts and ideas make you who you are and that is okay!

Believe in yourself—you truly can be whatever you wish!

—*Laura Pearce, MEd, Elementary Education*
(she/her/hers)
Author, Educator, Grandparent

Letter from a Grown-up Trans Girl

I'm a transgender high school student. When I was born, my parents thought I was a boy. Growing up, I was very feminine. Whenever I had the chance, I dressed up in my friends' skirts and dresses. Whenever a group was separated into boys and girls, I convinced my teacher to let me be with the girls.

Back then, I didn't have the resources to help with my identity exploration. By the time I was twelve, I heard about a famous transgender woman and realized for the first time that there were nonbinary options. It gave me the courage to come out as transgender and to change my name.

Fortunately, I grew up in a supportive environment. My family didn't try to control my decisions around gender and allowed me to explore and make my own choices. As someone going through this, my advice for any friend or family member is to try to understand that this is *their* journey. I think the most important thing is to provide the love and acceptance we all need to have the confidence to fully express ourselves.

—Aria
(she/her/hers)

Letter from a Family

They say that children are our greatest teachers and raising our son has proved that time and time again. Our gender journey began when our son was only three years old, and the last three years have taught us so much.

When he told us in his little toddler voice that he was NOT a girl, he was as clear as day. As parents in the queer community, we thought we had everything figured out and knew what was next. It turned out that we didn't know much about gender identity and expression and had a LOT to learn.

We have let our son lead the way, affirming his choices and answering his questions the best we can. We have had to educate ourselves and find resources for those around us. Because even though most kids understand and accept all sorts of gender identity and expression among their peers, adults are usually way behind.

Having books and articles was helpful for us as parents, but having a variety of children's books is and was even more important. Helping gender-expansive children have the language and terminology for their peers is empowering and helps their confidence, and seeing themselves in books is critical! Especially at young ages, it is so important for kids' books to reflect the world around them. The more books that show kids there are many ways to be a kid, the better! If we set the foundation for acceptance and inclusion early, it is so much easier as they grow up.

Authors' Note

We hope our book will help all children become aware that they are part of a diverse interconnectedness. In this book, we have interviewed a wide range of kids about their gender identities and recorded and transcribed their responses. We've used their own words to raise up their voices, to show how much we have in common and how truly unique we each are.

Figuring out who we are in the world has its challenges. Young children are trying to make sense of, interpret, and organize their world as they grow and develop in their own way. In our culture, we have traditionally been born into a binary world defined by two genders—either boy or girl.

That way of being defined is shifting. More and more kids are identifying as genderfluid, gender nonconforming, or nonbinary, that is, genders that are not exclusively male or female.

As educators, we knew there was a need for a book about gender identity for this young age range, and that the topic would need to be approached with loving kindness, promoting acceptance, inclusivity, and representation for all children. We wanted our work to help dismantle biased cultural and social stereotypes that unfairly perpetuate myths that promote conformity over creativity, and the gender binary over gender expansiveness. We worked with many experts in the field as well as with transgender and gender nonconforming sensitivity readers. We relied on their knowledge, expertise, and lived experiences as we wrote this book. And most importantly, we listened to the real experts—the kids who shared their stories. We would love for this book to serve as a catalyst for reflective conversation for children and grown-ups alike.

—*Gwen and Shelley*

A Introduction for Caregivers, Educators, and Loved Ones of Children on the Gender Spectrum

TRUST AND RESPECT

Kids know themselves best. Let things unfold in their own time. Teach them that they are the sole expert concerning their gender.

ENVIRONMENT

Create a loving, supportive, and safe space at home for your child's gender exploration by providing books, wall decor, dress-up clothes, art supplies, and figures for role-play. This supports inclusivity and diversity. Have gender-neutral bathrooms and use nonbinary terms to form lines and groups.

READ

Sharing books that include nonbinary, genderfluid, and transgender characters will help kids to reflect, identify, and perhaps allow them to express their feelings. You can always interchange names or pronouns when reading. Check with schools and local libraries to find books with gender diversity.

EDUCATE

Try to learn as much as you can about the gender spectrum and appropriate pronouns. By becoming more informed, you will become more comfortable and the children will too. Look for workshops, trainings, and podcasts for your colleagues and community to become more informed and to help educate others.

PRONOUNS

People of different gender identities use different pronouns to refer to how they like to be addressed. Some folks use "he" or "she," but others may use "they" or "ze." Some people use all pronouns or multiple sets of pronouns. It's better to ask than assume which pronouns people use. Sometimes gendered ways to address people like "Mom" and "Dad" are replaced by gender-neutral options like "parent(s)," "Maddy," and "Gaga."

LANGUAGE MATTERS

While language is evolving on a day-to-day basis and we realize that some terminology will become dated, it's important to continue to educate ourselves and use the right words.

TRANSGENDER TERMINOLOGY SUGGESTIONS

He is transgender.

Incorrect

He is a transgender.

She transitioned a few years ago.

Incorrect

She transgendered a few years ago.

They transitioned.

Incorrect

They changed genders.

Before he transitioned . . .

Incorrect

Before he became a boy . . .

Gender identity and sexual orientation are not the same.

Incorrect

Being trans means you're gay.

Don't ask about surgeries/private parts unless a person explicitly invites that conversation!

Incorrect

Did you get the surgery?

When he presented as a woman/a girl . . .

Incorrect

When he was a women/a girl . . .

COMMUNITY

Bringing adults and children of all genders into your life can help normalize gender variance. Make connections through schools, neighborhoods, churches, synagogues, and mosques. Nonbinary, genderfluid, and transgender actors, artists, sports figures, and elected officials can help serve as role models.

LOVE

Embrace different forms of self-expression so your child can have a healthy start early in their life. Let them know you love them for who they are.

Therapeutic Support

When a child's emerging gender identity is unexpected, parents may wonder how best to support their development. Families can begin by finding a trusted medical care provider that is actively affirming and has a history of working with trans and gender nonconforming people. Therapeutic support can help build a support system and community network that can honor and celebrate gender expansiveness. Parents may need the support even more than the children.

According to experts, children begin to consolidate an understanding of gender identity between two and five years of age. They may have questions about the similarities and differences between their bodies and their parents' bodies, or about who has a penis, who has a vagina, neither, or both. It's common for children to "try on" different roles on a diverse spectrum of gender journey possibilities.

When children are supported in exploring their fluidity and creativity that is beautifully unique to each work as caregivers is to create a loving, respectful, and with unlimited possibilities so that children have the freedom in and through gendered worlds, discovering different gender e pronouns, and felt identities. These moments are many, like snapshots expressions and experiences that ebb and flow with gender development.

—Shannon L. Sennott, LICSW
(she/her/he

Introductory Glossary

AFAB: stands for "assigned female at birth."

agender: denoting or relating to a person who does not identify themselves as having a particular gender.

AMAB: stands for "assigned male at birth."

cisgender: an adjective that describes someone who identifies with the gender they were assigned at birth.

deadname: refers to the name someone was given or used before they transitioned and/or discovered their true gender identity.

dysphoria: the discomfort or distress that arises from the incongruence of gender identity and gender assigned at birth.

FTM: stands for "female to male" and refers to people assigned female at birth but who identify as male. Some folks dislike this term because it implies that someone was once female, which can be inaccurate.

gender binary: a system of gender classification that says there are only two fixed genders, either male or female, man or woman.

gender euphoria: a feeling of joy that a transgender or nonbinary person can have when they think about, feel, and/or are affirmed by their true gender identity.

gender expression: how individuals communicate their gender to others.

genderfluid: a person whose gender identity is not fixed.

gender identity: an individual's personal sense of having a particular gender. This does not have to match "biological sex."

gender-neutral: suitable for, applicable to, all genders.

genderqueer: an umbrella term for people who do not subscribe to conventional gender distinctions but identify with neither, both, or a combination of genders.

gender spectrum: the many different gender identities, including agender, transgender, nonbinary, genderqueer, genderfluid, and cisgender.

intersex: a term that a person may use when they have both male and female sex characteristics.

MTF: stands for "male to female" and refers to people assigned male at birth but who identify as female. Some folks dislike this term because it implies that someone was once male, which can be inaccurate.

nibling: a gender-neutral term used to refer to a child of one's sibling as a replacement for "niece" or "nephew."

nonbinary: an umbrella term, similar to genderqueer, for folks who identify outside of the gender binary.

pibling: a gender-neutral term used to refer to either an aunt or an uncle that is modeled on the word "sibling," blended with the "p" from "parent."

pronouns: words that take the place of proper nouns. She/her/hers, they/them/theirs, and he/him/his are more common pronouns, but neopronouns like ze/hir/hirs and ey/em/eirs are also used by gender nonconforming people.

queer: of, relating to, or being a person whose sexual orientation is not heterosexual and/or whose gender identity is not cisgender.

transfeminine (or transfemme): a person who was assigned male at birth but identifies as more feminine.

transgender: an adjective for someone who does not identify with the gender they were assigned at birth.

transition: any step(s) a person takes to affirm their gender identity. This may or may not include changes in one's name, pronouns, physical appearance, or clothing; taking hormones; and undergoing surgery, among many other things. There is no one way to transition.

trans man: a person who was assigned female at birth but identifies as male.

transmasculine (or transmasc): a person who was assigned female at birth but identifies as more masculine.

trans woman: a person who was assigned male at birth but identifies as female.

Resources & Sources

Websites

brandeis.edu
Checklist for the Gender-Inclusive Classroom: The checklist from Brandeis University offers concrete suggestions on how to create a gender-inclusive classroom.

genderinclassrooms.com/inclusive-curriculum
Curriculum welcoming gender-inclusive classrooms.

genderwheel.com
Curriculum and educational tools expanding gender discussions with intersectional, anti-oppression, community-centered perspectives in a social justice framework by Maya Gonzalez.

glsen.org
Working to ensure that every member of every school community is valued and respected regardless of sexual orientation, gender identity, or gender expression.

learningforjustice.org
Includes Lesson Plans on Gender Equity and Lesson Plan on Gender Expression

naeyc.org
Children's Books That Break Gender Role Stereotypes: An annotated list of recommended children's books that challenge traditional notions of gender and inspiring stories for the classroom from the National Association for the Education of Young Children.

pinkmantaray.com
Schuyler Bailar is the first trans athlete to compete in any sport on an NCAA D1 men's team, and the only one to have competed for all four years. He is an internationally celebrated inspirational speaker and a respected advocate for inclusion, body acceptance, and mental health awareness.

teachunicef.org
Gender Equality Teaching Plans: From UNICEF. This collection of teacher resources, including units, lesson plans, videos, multimedia, and stories, is intended to raise student awareness of the importance of gender equality. Useful for giving a global perspective to the issue.

transparentUSA.org
TransParent is an organization envisioning a world that affirms the naturally occurring transgender experience with compassionate support to navigate complex issues.

Building your Family Library

A Quick and Easy Guide to They/Them Pronouns
by Archie Bongiovanni and Tristan Jimerson

Beyond the Gender Binary
by Alok Vaid-Menon

Raising the Transgender Child: A Complete Guide for Parents, Families, and Caregivers
by Michele Angello and Ali Bowman

Trans-Kin: A Guide for Family and Friends of Transgender People
edited by Eleanor A. Hubbard and Cameron T. Whitley

Dedicated to the beautiful children and the families who have shared their expansive and inclusive experiences with gender, ranging from transgender to genderfluid to cisgender to nonbinary and beyond. The kids and caregivers were photographed and their words were recorded at a moment in time with the full understanding that their gender exploration might be fluid and change day by day.

—*G.A. and S.R.*

Clarion Books is an imprint of HarperCollins Publishers.
True You
Text copyright © 2022 by Gwen Agna and Shelley Rotner
Photographs copyright © 2022 by Shelley Rotner

ISBN 978-0-06-324046-9

Typography by Stephanie Hays

22 23 24 25 26 RTLO 10 9 8 7 6 5 4 3 2 1

First Edition